Yesterday Is Only a Memory

MICHAEL MOORE

PAGE PUBLISHING, INC.
New York, NY

First originally published by Page Publishing, Inc. 2014

ISBN 978-1-63417-246-2 (pbk)
ISBN 978-1-63417-247-9 (digital)

Printed in the United States of America

My Succubus

Realization of facts secrets withheld.
I can't escape from your created hell.
I may have failed, but you went so extreme.
Destroyed all hope stealing my dreams.
Venom-laced words that sounded so sweet.
I couldn't dissect your lines, find your deceit.
It all came out, your wrath unleashed,
Godly destruction in need of a priest.
Now I'm searching to answer my prayers,
Digging deeper and deeper unraveling layers.
This answer I'm searching, can't seem to find.
Keep looking and hoping. All I have is time.
If time runs out, I guess that I fail.
Now walking through rain that turned to hail.
Survive 'cause I must, can't afford to quit.
Life must go on. Time to forget the bullshit.

Me

What I want. What I expect. I don't know.
What I need. What I crave. I can't show.
What I am. What I do. I can't hide.
What I show. What I have is pride.
What I lack. What I lost is you.
What I fear. Why I flee is truth.

Blind myself by what I think I need.
Life of wanting is filled with greed.
I close my thoughts to what I have.
So simple and stupid, I'm forced to laugh.
Keep running away from the truth that I face.
Need to push through, no need for disgrace.
Man up and face what I have become.
Need to open my eyes, accept where I'm from.

I can't escape my past or keep hiding scars.
Life happens so fast, blown too many pars.
Time to move ahead and admit to my flaws,
Before I end up dead, taken by regret's claws.

Afraid to be abandoned and left all alone.
Afraid I am nothing more than just a drone.
I talk to myself, not convinced I'm the best.
Truth is, I'm just as flawed as all the rest.
I'm silent by choice, nothing great to say.
Confidence nonexistent. Price I had to pay.

MICHAEL MOORE

I bottle up emotions until they overflow.
People get too close, that's when I tend to blow.

I can't escape my past or keep hiding scars.
Life happens so fast, blown too many pars.
Time to move ahead and admit to my flaws,
Before I end up dead, taken by regret's claws.

Feel It Every Moment

Can you smell it? Can you feel it in the air?
Or are you too far gone to even care?
It hangs so thick. It's hard to breathe!
Can't avoid what's carried by the breeze.

It's love that I'm feeling. I'm alone and unsure.
Love is painful. I wish I had a cure.
Shared love, the greatest feeling ever.
One-way love, torture that lasts forever.

I feel like I'm wrapped in a boa's embrace.
Getting tighter and tighter with each image I face.
Heart's ready to burst. My stomach in knots.
Why am I not the one that you want?
I'll give you all that I have and more than I can.
Just take me away. Let me be your man.

It's love that I'm feeling. I'm alone and unsure.
Love is painful. I wish I had a cure.
Shared love, the greatest feeling ever.
One-way love, torture that lasts forever.

MICHAEL MOORE

View from Above

This moment monumental in time.
Get a step ahead or fall behind.
Does it matter where you end your stride?
Or is it about the thrills you endure on this ride?

You go through life to search for a way to succeed.
And miss all the joy to be had in uncertainty.
The thrill of the unknown is a rush to be had.
No plans for the future, is that really so bad?
Does it really matter if you never set a trend?
The ride keeps moving. We all know where it ends.

This moment monumental in time.
Get a step ahead or fall behind.
Does it matter where you end your stride?
Or is it about the thrills you endure on this ride?

Optimize your options and let go of your stress.
No use to worry. Life can only end in death.
Is that really so grim? Is there no need to be high?
Success is being able to smile the moment you die.
So live in the moment and make the best of each one.
Be sure to have no regrets when this life is done.

This moment monumental in time.
Get a step ahead or fall behind.
Does it matter where you end your stride?
Or is it about the thrills you endure on this ride?

Hopefully optimistic is such a way to be.
Altering your view of this thing called reality.
The gloom just won't keep you down.
Your smile never replaced by a frown.
Feel your floating above the ground.
Feet moving not making a sound.
Floating away. Freedom bound.
Your dream's in reach! Don't turn around.

So Far Gone

Far away, but not so far gone.
We will meet again. It won't be too long.
Distance pushes and pulls us apart.
Nothing will ever take you away from my heart.
While moments pass and time runs by.
Always remember that I'll be your guy.

Although you can't see me. It doesn't mean I'm not there.
Just because I don't call doesn't mean I don't care.
Not a moment goes by that you're not on my mind.
To hear your voice makes this harder each time.

In a fortress of solitude 'cause I must be.
Much time will pass before I am free.
What I want is you, but for now I can't touch.
To hear you want the same is just too much.
There's too much to handle. Break down these walls.
If only I could. I just don't have the balls.

Although you can't see me. It doesn't mean I'm not there.
Just because I don't call doesn't mean I don't care.
Not a moment goes by that you're not on my mind.
To hear your voice makes this harder each time.

I talk a big game, but inside I am weak.
I wonder if I'm the one you truly seek.

Self-doubt is to never try thus never fail.
Self-preservation is being too afraid to set sail.
There are traits I have and wish to lose.
Maybe then I will finally make a move.

MICHAEL MOORE

Freedom Is a Cell

I'm alive, so I'm going to live.
Life's too short, yet the world's so big.
The options are endless, the opportunity's there.
Love's perfect hand is running through flawless hair.
A sunrise atop a mountain. A sunset on the beach.
There's only one thing wrong. Love is out of reach.

These things I don't do. I'm waiting, you see?
These things are much better when part of a we.
I thought for so long to be alone meant to be free.
It's just a different prison that is surrounding me.

The tank is on empty in the middle of the woods.
Though with that special person, life still feels good.
Loneliness is fearful and dark on a bright sunny day.
The color's all blurry into a sad shade of grey.
Every noise seems much closer than the last.
Imagining a predator approaching me fast.

These things I don't do. I'm waiting, you see?
These things are much better when part of a we.
I thought for so long to be alone meant to be free.
It's just a different prison that is surrounding me.

Where are you the love of my life?
Why won't you come and end my strife?
Did you take a wrong turn and forget to look back?
Or did you realize that I am too much of a hack?

Are you waiting and asking the same questions as me?
Do you need me to find you, so we can be free?

These things I don't do. I'm waiting, you see?
These things are much better when part of a we.
I thought for so long to be alone meant to be free.
It's just a different prison that is surrounding me.

Transformation of a Soul

Beyond all hope, just short of fear.
The moment just before shedding tears.
You're standing in limbo, though not sure why.
Wishing so bad you were learning to fly.
You want to escape but cannot move away.
Swear to yourself that you'll get out some day.

Promise yourself a million times.
That you'll find a way to break these vines.
The night is darkest just before dawn.
But when day breaks, you may be long gone.

Beyond all fear, so far from hope.
Your hands tense while slitting your throat.
It can break you down for no reason at all.
Push you off the edge just to watch you fall.
The world is against all dreams that you have
It is a black hole, sucking away the joy you once had.

Promise yourself a million times.
That you'll find a way to break these vines.
The night is darkest just before dawn.
But when day breaks, you may be long gone.

Beyond emotions, you no longer care.
Everyone you see can't help but glare.
You dare them to say one thing to piss you off.
You've become so cold. It's too painful being soft.

Make them feel the pain that made you change.
You felt too much torment then became deranged.

It broke you down one too many times.
You are now those strangling vines.
The night's growing darker, there's no hope for dawn.
There is no day break. You are too far gone.

Fortune Cookie

Too often my meanings are misunderstood.
Do you understand me? I wish you could.
Break me open like a fortune cookie.
The answer is there. It's not too tricky.
I'm outside the box, but inside your mind.
Searching for a reason to waste my time.

Can you understand the feelings I feel?
I'm just a banana waiting to be peeled.
A knight waiting for a reason to kneel.
A fishing rod that's missing its reel.
Can you relate to these feelings I feel?
Look into your eyes, but I can't tell what is real.
Someone must stop these feelings I feel.

Do you understand? I don't think that you can.
Though you say you do, I'm a furnace with no fan.
I've got power to warm, but no way to spread.
You misunderstand. It's all in my head.
That's where you're wrong and what I hate.
Maybe it's not in my head, it is actually fate.

Can you understand the feelings I feel?
I'm just a banana waiting to be peeled.
A knight waiting for a reason to kneel.
A fishing rod that's missing it's reel.
Can you relate to these feelings I feel?

Look into your eyes, but I can't tell what is real.
Someone must stop these feelings I feel.

Alone now. A feeling that will last forever.
Accepting this fate will make it better.
Tired of trying. Tired of hoping.
So tired of these dreams of eloping.
Each day I wake up with hopes that it's better.
In truth those dreams I want to arise will never.

MICHAEL MOORE

Vanishing Dream

She comes to me at night.
Beyond all pain she holds me tight.
A chest on which I release my tears
Her hand strokes my head, calming my fears.
The perfect feeling. We fit just right.
Where are you now? Always gone after the night.

Dream lady, my upscale baby.
There is no chance for debating.
Hold me now. Don't ever let go.
Can't control these feelings I know.
Please, please I beg you! Don't ever let go.

Beyond all hope. Morning comes and you're gone.
I feel like the only fish in a dried up pond.
Black wind blowing. Cold air down my lungs.
Seems the rest of the world only speaks in tongues.
I shatter a mirror. The reflection more accurate.
I'm broken is the simple fact of it.

Dream lady, my upscale baby.
There is no chance for debating.
Hold me now. Don't ever let go.
Can't control these feelings I know.
Please, please I beg you! Don't ever let go.

Killing myself searching the world for you.
Without you, I'm a car with no fuel.

A book with no words. A tree with no roots.
A plane with no wings. A blind man getting looks.
I make no sense. Have no senses without you.
Everything blurs to a riddle with no clue.

Dream lady, my upscale baby.
There is no chance for debating.
Hold me now. Don't ever let go.
Can't control these feelings I know.
Please, please I beg you! Don't ever let go.

MICHAEL MOORE

The Inevitable

Let's start this over. Become something new.
Just take it from the top. It's all we can do.
I messed up I know. You know you did too.
Let's start this over. Become something true.

Where did this go wrong? When did it all start?
When was this first time that I broke your heart?
When did you cry? Too often I fear.
Why do you flinch every time I come near?
I never hit you. You know I never would.
I know I messed up, but this can still be good.

Let's start this over. Become something new.
Just take it from the top. It's all we can do.
I messed up I know. You know you did too.
Let's start this over. Become something true.

I can forgive what you've done and try to forget.
Or is it to the point where we just shouldn't fret?
Have my hands lost their warmth, sending chills down your spine?
Please, baby, just tell me. Why is it you cry?
I cannot let you go. Don't you feel the same?
I know you're leaving. This feels like a game.

Let's start this over. Become something new.
Just take it from the top. It's all we can do.
I messed up I know. You know you did too.
Let's start this over. Become something true.

I will keep in touch somehow, some way.
I'll still think of you every dreary day.
That's how it will stay until you return.
I'm standing in a fire, but I can't feel the burn.
Without you, there's no feeling, inside or out.
I'm a flower in a meadow dying from a drought.

All for You

So sweet and inviting this image I see.
So warm and soothing. It's confusing me.
Breaking my will and drawing me in.
Is this my chance? Will I have it again?
Am I ready? Or just kidding myself?
Oh what a hand my fate has dealt.

Should I jump in and go for the gold?
Take this risk or stay within my mold?
This could be it. Maybe it's worth a shot,
But then again, what if it's not?

When we talk I feel I could fly.
So much excitement. I feel I could die.
Truth is reality can be a bitch.
Like striking out from a wicked fast pitch.
Can my fantasies become reality?
Or am I just heading for another fatality?

Should I jump in and go for the gold?
Take this risk or stay within my mold?
This could be it. Maybe it's worth a shot,
But then again, what if it's not?

Happiness is a warm gun.
I question if it's only meant for some.
Sugar pie. Honey bunch.
Life seems more a sucker punch.

Now you do that thing you do.
Where you break my heart in two.
Let's not forget. Love me do.
Babe all I want is to love you.

Should I jump in and go for the gold?
Take this risk or stay within my mold?
This could be it. Maybe it's worth a shot,
But then again, what if it's not?

Inspired by a Dream

Goddamn. I hate this shit!
I put up with too much. I'm fucking done with it!
Led me astray again and again.
Here to tell you. This is the end.
Done searching and hoping I'm on the right path.
Fail once. Fail twice. You do the math.
It doesn't add up. I'm tired of the pain.
I'm sad every day for sunshine looks just like rain.

Great remorse. No sensual bliss.
Mixed up and broke down. I pray for a kiss.
A hug. To be touched. I feel so deprived.
Anything to make me feel somewhat alive.

Reaching out for what I have no clue.
Is there any way to cure an emotional bruise?
Emotional wrong word, more like I don't know.
Can't describe what I can't define, no linguistic pro.
Feel like a sloth keep waiting to make a move.
But the world's too far ahead, a race I'm bound to lose.

Great remorse. No sensual bliss.
Mixed up and broke down. I pray for a kiss.
A hug. To be touched. I feel so deprived.
Anything to make me feel somewhat alive.

I make a move. Though it feels like a mistake.
Sends me to a vortex from which there's no escape.

This black hole keeps pulling harder each day.
Feels so close now. I think it's here to stay.
It follows me down this path called life.
It riddles my being with nothing but strife.

Great remorse. No sensual bliss.
Mixed up and broke down. I pray for a kiss.
A hug. To be touched. I feel so deprived.
Anything to make me feel somewhat alive.

For the People I Love

Sitting in the burning rays of the sun.
Counting the hours until I'm done.
I go home to nothing. That's just my luck.
I'm lost in my head. No one gives a fuck.
They don't care about what matters or what's coming next.
They don't care whose life they shatter. It just makes no sense.

I don't say it enough. I don't know why.
There is something I must get off my mind.
To everyone who thinks of me.
To everyone I rarely see.
I will say it. It's way past due.
I'm so very proud to love you.

I've never been great at keeping tabs.
I'm not the type to pick up the phone and gab.
That doesn't mean I don't think of you.
Hearing your voice cuts me deep. It's true.
Fills me up with sadness and memories of the days.
When we would hang together just soaking up rays.

I don't say it enough. I don't know why.
There is something I must get off my mind.
To everyone who thinks of me.
To everyone I rarely see.
I will say it. It's way past due.
I'm so very proud to love you.

Sweet Memories

Memories come rushing back to me.
Opened my eyes to a new world to see.
Things were so great. They seldom were bad.
But life tore apart the love that we had.
Those memories still linger on.
Always there. Even when you're gone.

My mind is flooded by thoughts of what could have been.
My pulse is racing at the thought of seeing you again.
The one that had me floating so high in the air.
The one to this day who I know to still care.

Was it puppy love or something more in depth?
It had to be more than the pain felt when I left.
The pain I remember to this very day.
The scar that left me shaking and searching for a way.
The memories that keep me from soaring above.
A way to forget this thing they call love.

My mind is flooded by thoughts of what could have been.
My pulse is racing at the thought of seeing you again.
The one that had me floating so high in the air.
The one to this day who I know to still care.

MICHAEL MOORE

Intervention

Operation intervention.
Grab a friend for resurrection.
Someone who once cared.
Someone who is now just too impaired.
A life you see slowly slipping to nothing.
Stand up, be a friend, and do something.

Everyone slips. Some people they fall.
Save them! Be a man and grow some balls!
It takes so little; seems like nothing at all.
Reach out and grab hold! There's no time to stall.

You see them every day.
Walking like zombies. Their life slipping away.
A "druggie," an "alchy," an addict to bad situations.
A person worth loving, but surrounded by bad motivations.
Their health is slipping and spiraling downhill.
Losing track of the days and their past due bills.

Everyone slips. Some people they fall.
Save them! Be a man and grow some balls!
It takes so little; seems like nothing at all.
Reach out and grab hold! There's no time to stall.

Not your problem? Have you no heart?
A life ruined by addictions from the very start.

Can't forget the most priceless image to see.
A look in the mirror is the power to set you free.
Because everyone is special it is in you to try.
Or you can watch a life wasted as you walk on by.

Just Another Dream

It's time to put a smile on.
View the world from a pylon.
Nevermore to be discouraged.
Moving forward to a world less deserted.
Never to want more, just giving a little less.
I have a secret and it's time to confess.

This world keeps spinning from now to forever
Promise to hold you for just as long.
If you're my girl. I will leave you never.
Baby we could be a love song.

Electricity running through my veins.
I keep on praying it doesn't rain.
I keep waiting for this surge to subside.
It's hard to write this. It crushes my pride.
But girl till you're by my side.
This energy will be stuck inside.

This world keeps spinning from now to forever
Promise to hold you for just as long.
If you're my girl. I will leave you never.
Baby we could be a love song.

Just hold me and never let me go.
This hard, rough exterior is just a show.
I melt to your touch like butter in a pan.
Just like a groupie. Babe, I'm your biggest fan.

Faith is overflowing; flowing over me.
Secret is, there is no one else I'd rather see.

This world keeps spinning from now to forever
Promise to hold you for just as long.
If you're my girl. I will leave you never.
Baby we could be a love song.

Tamable Beast

Do you believe in fate?
Can you cure heartbreak?
Have you made mistakes?
Will you smile for my sake?
Tell me! Can you cure my heartbreak?

I've left people bloody and broken.
Through words I should never have spoken.
Spouts of rage bursting to ease my pain.
Leaving bystanders in unspoken disdain.
My smile was just a cover.
I never meant to crush any of my brothers.
These feelings inside keep boiling and expanding.
Body feels like an explosion just short of happening.
Can you ease this pressure?
Take all this pain, or make it lesser?
Or am I stuck to cope all alone?
Walking through life, nothing more than a drone.

Do you believe in fate?
Can you cure heartbreak?
Have you made mistakes?
Will you smile for my sake?
Tell me! Can you cure my heartbreak?

Run and hide if you fear this beast.
Run away child or you shall be his feast.

A victim of his hearts own desires.
A victim left broken, yet inspired.
So run! Run, as fast as you can!
Unless you have the strength to save this man.
Because if you believe in fate.
Then you may cure this heartbreak.
Make no mistake.
I need you to smile for my sake.
For you may be the only cure for my heartbreak.

Undeservingly Deserving

An exchange of numbers, no exchange of fates.
He just can't make the call to arrange a date.
He will think and ponder and ask himself, why?
Who would want this ordinary guy?
She's exquisite! Amazing! She's such a beauty!
He's just a supporting actor in your movie.

The guy in the background who's full of "one-liners."
The girl in the foreground, never seen someone finer.
He picks up the phone and slams it back down.
He's got no chance with the finest girl in town.

She's sitting at home hoping and praying.
Waiting for a call from the guy worth dating.
Tired of assholes and all of their friends.
Wants the guy who never follows trends.
But he isn't calling and she wonders, why?
Why she's undeserving of this perfect guy?

The girl in the spotlight now feeling so broken.
The guy out of sight who's feeling unspoken.
She lies in her bed. The tears start to flow.
He tells himself it's time to just let go.

Pages in a Book

I need your help to feel alive.
For too many years I've felt dead inside.
A corpse hidden by these breaths I'm taking.
It's the perfect cover. There is no mistaking.
But deep down within I need to feel again.
I'm playing solo in this game I cannot win.

Take my hand, girl. Now don't be shy.
I need your strength. Let's take a ride.
No place to go now. Baby, let's just drive.
If I were your man. I'd feel so alive!

My blood is rushing right to my face.
You got me blushing. Wanting a taste!
Feeling more alive than ever before.
You got me wishing and hoping for more.
Counting the hours till I see you again.
Baby, we could be the next Barbie and Ken.

Take my hand, girl. Now don't be shy.
I need your strength. Let's take a ride.
No place to go now. Baby, let's just drive.
If I were your man. I'd feel so alive!

Tell me that this story will never end.
I'm feeling like Atreyu. It just starts again.

MICHAEL MOORE

You know you're my empress in a crystal tower.
Come with me, baby. You know you got the power.
To end all this sadness in this world of mine.
Pages keep on turning. We're running out of time.

Floating Away

In her eyes I see who I want to be.
The man she lays with is worry-free.
In her eyes I see my future, not my past.
The first lips I will kiss to be my last.
In her eyes my troubles float away.
My darkest nights become my brightest days.

Feet barely touching the ground.
Floating away not making a sound.
Making me want to be more than I am.
She's taking me to a more beautiful land.

When she smiles my heart melts away.
Please tell me, sweetie, you're here to stay.
When she smiles dreams become reality.
Sadness fades. Feels like immortality.
When she smiles my anger fades away.
Words can't describe what I'm trying to say.

Feet barely touching the ground.
Floating away not making a sound.
Making me want to be more than I am.
She's taking me to a more beautiful land.

The way she moves could make a blind man blush.
She's able to make a calm man's blood rush.

The way she moves is graceful and pure.
No man could be immune to her lure.
The way she moves can cause all to stutter.
You know I think I may just love her.

Dream Girl

Somebody wake me. I must be dreaming.
Seems too perfect. My eyes are deceiving.
One look at this girl and I stopped breathing.
One touch of her hand my heart stopped beating.
Time slows down. I take in this perfect scene.
Somebody wake me. It must be a dream.

Perfection like this cannot be real.
I must have made a devilish deal.
To her beauty I'm forced to kneel.
My heart is hers, that she did steal.
For a glance at her I would give up my last meal.

Please don't wake me. I don't want this dream to end.
Reality leaves me with nothing to defend.
If this is not real my heart could never mend.
Stuck in hell. My soul twisted and forced to bend.
I have a message for you to send.
Don't wake me. This dream can never end.

Perfection like this cannot be real.
I must have made a devilish deal.
To her beauty I'm forced to kneel.
My heart is hers, which she did steal.
For a glance at her I would give up my last meal.

My eyes wide open. The dream has passed.
Reality sinks in for me to grasp.

MICHAEL MOORE

I know she is out there. I need to find her fast.
The race to her heart, I cannot finish in last.
If I do, I'll be forced to kick my own ass.
For my eyes are wide open and that dream has passed.

Tough Times

Drunken thoughts forming shattering lies.
Everyone wonders why is it she cries?
Her heart has been broken by thoughts so impure.
Now she lies searching and reaching for a cure.
Never can remember. Never will forget.
What happened and where that relationship went?

She takes another sip.
She's starting to tip.
She takes another drink.
Says it helps her think.
One last shot to ease the pain.
Drinking away her life. What a shame.

On the outside, she is a riot.
Life of the party. She never is quiet.
The more she consumes, the wider she smiles.
Sometimes it seems like it goes on for miles.
But when the morning comes and drunk is done.
No smile remains. Life is not all fun.

She takes another sip.
She's starting to tip.
She takes another drink.
Says it helps her think.
One last shot to ease the pain.
Drinking away her life. What a shame.

MICHAEL MOORE

Friends ask her, "What is wrong?
Why, oh why, is your face so long?"
"Nothing's the matter everything is fine.
I have some problems, but you know they are mine.
I'll have a drink. It will all be good."
Pride is a killer wish she had understood.

She takes another sip.
She's starting to tip.
She takes another drink.
Says it helps her think.
One last shot to ease the pain.
Drinking away her life. What a shame.

Forgive or Forget

My eyes are open. I fear this no more.
Never going to forget how you set the score.
Competitive is what we always were.
To win you did something so impure.
You left me a broken fragile mess.
Wondering if you truly were the best.

Friend becomes enemy.
Tore me apart.
You were no friend to me.
You aided in breaking my heart.
Obsolete is how I felt.
An ice cube about to melt.
Left me crying in the rain.
Watching as I swirled down the drain.

Our fun and games became life and death.
You betrayed me with that devastating theft.
The one thing I had that kept on pushing me through.
You snuck in at night and took it. I didn't have a clue.
I'll never forget that image burned inside.
I'll never forget the night you should have died.

Friend becomes enemy.
Tore me apart.
You were no friend to me.
You aided in breaking my heart.

MICHAEL MOORE

Obsolete is how I felt.
An ice cube about to melt.
Left me crying in the rain.
Watching as I swirled down the drain.

Heartless for Breaking Hearts

You think I am the one who shall not be named?
The lord of darkness, hatred, and pain?
Because I saved you from the destruction I would cause.
Does that make me the demon with wide open jaws?
Am I happy for the times that I made you cry?
Don't you know it killed me when I said good-bye?

Believe I have no heart an empty shell.
I love the fact that I put you through hell.
It was my goal from the start, I guess.
I never felt any pain in my chest.
Heart is covered by an emotion-proof vest.
If that's what you want to believe. Then be my guest.

You think I walk this earth to just shatter hearts.
Crunch, grind, and destroy every little part.
Believe I'm the epitome of emotional destruction.
If that will begin your emotional reconstruction.
I did what I did to protect you from me.
At that point in your life, I was just a disease.

Believe I have no heart an empty shell.
I love the fact that I put you through hell.
It was my goal from the start, I guess.
I never felt any pain in my chest.
Heart is covered by an emotion-proof vest.
If that's what you want to believe. Then be my guest.

MICHAEL MOORE

The Deception of a Storm

Roll out of bed, and stumble through my dorm.
I love waking up to the sound of a storm.
It's like nature's little drum set, music to my ears.
With the cleansing rain making everything so clear.
The trees are swaying to the music at hand.
The leaves are fluttering, adding to nature's band.

Trickle. Crash. Boom. Rustle.
Listen close to nature's hustle.
Rustle. Boom. Crash. Trickle
Standing so close to death's sickle.
Trickle. Crash. Rustle. Boom.
Nature's music could bring your doom.
Boom. Rustle. Trickle. Crash.
Listen from a distance to save your ass.

A storm's beauty can be deceiving.
Careful else your family will end up grieving.
One small crash could bring your final breath.
One fallen tree could bring your death.
You should listen from a good distance away.
So you can live to hear natures song another day.

Trickle. Crash. Boom. Rustle.
Listen close to nature's hustle.
Rustle. Boom. Crash. Trickle
Standing so close to death's sickle.

Trickle. Crash. Rustle. Boom.
Nature's music could bring your doom.
Boom. Rustle. Trickle. Crash.
Listen from a distance to save your ass.

Wind picks up and trees can no longer be trusted.
Hail pouring down leaving everything busted.
The climax is here. The fury unleashed.
Better hope you have shelter from this beast.
If not your story is over. There is no tomorrow.
Just as the storm calms down as if showing you sorrow.

MICHAEL MOORE

Shell-shocked

Her smile could end depression; shatter the strongest of wills.
The sound of her voice can give an orchestra chills.
Her curves more dangerous than a hairpin at eighty.
One look. No going back. No chance of debating.
A visual masterpiece a personality to match.
If only I knew a way to start this romance.

I'm so shell-shocked. I can't move forward.
Shell-shocked has my confidence lowered.
My mind is a twisted mess when she's around.
Takes all of my courage to just make a sound.

Anything I'm good at, I can't do when she's standing near.
Concentration is nonexistent, I fear.
I was an ace before, now performing like a chum.
The smoothest road once traveled, now I'm hitting every bump.
Got to find an answer, away to break this trance.
I might, if only, I could ask her for a dance.

I'm so shell-shocked. I can't move forward.
Shell-shocked has my confidence lowered.
My mind is a twisted mess when she's around.
Takes all of my courage to just make a sound.

Words once rolled off my tongue with ease.
Now I'm stuttering over words as easy as please.
Once stood proud, now I'm down on my knees.
Shaking all over like I caught a disease.

Falling down so easy like wind struck trees.
Body is on fire. Why does my mind freeze?
She's killing me, man. She's such a tease.

I'm so shell-shocked. I can't move forward.
Shell-shocked has my confidence lowered.
My mind is a twisted mess when she's around.
Takes all of my courage to just make a sound.

About the Author

Michael Moore lives in the small, scenic town of Paradise, Michigan with his girlfriend, Lauren, dog, Shazam, and cat, Kitty Winks. He devotes his time to his two jobs, and also volunteers for the local fire department and ambulance core. He has five siblings, one older step-sister, two younger half-sisters, and two younger half-brothers. Michael enjoys sports, camping, music, playing his drums and just enjoying the little things in life. Writing also became a passion of his as a way of letting go of the pain and frustration that comes with life. He is looking forward to starting a family and starting the next step of this adventure.

CPSIA information can be obtained at www.ICGtesting.com
Printed in the USA
LVOW07s1514060715

444853LV00005B/21/P